BBC Gardeners'

POCK

SUMMER BEDDING

Andi Clevely

Photographs by Eric Crichton

BBC Books

Author Biography
Andi Clevely has been a working gardener for nearly thirty years. He began his career in Leeds City Council central nurseries and since then has worked in many gardens around the country, including Windsor Great Park. He is now responsible for a country estate and large garden in Stratford-on-Avon where he lives with his wife. Andi has written a number of gardening books and is a regular columnist for *Homes & Gardens* magazine.

Acknowledgements
The publishers would like to thank Colgrave Seeds, West Adderbury, Banbury, Oxfordshire for their assistance with the photography. Photographs on pages 8, 10, 11, 16, 19, 21, 22, 25, 28, 31, 34, 35, 37, 42, 44, 45, 46, 47, 48, 51, 55, 56, 58, 60, 61, 64, 65, 66, 67, 69, 72, 73, 77, 79 and 80 © Eric Crichton. All other photographs © BBC.

Published by BBC Books,
an imprint of BBC Worldwide Publishing.
BBC Worldwide Limited, Woodlands,
80 Wood Lane, London W12 0TT.

First published 1997
© BBC Worldwide Limited 1997
The moral right of the author has been asserted

ISBN 0 563 38777 7

Photographs by Eric Crichton

Set in Futura

Printed and bound in Belgium by Proost NV
Colour separations by Radstock Reproductions Limited, Midsomer Norton, Avon
Cover printed in Belgium by Proost NV

Common Names

INTRODUCTION

Bedding is all about seasonal colour, whether for winter, spring or summer flowering. For summer, there is a huge range of plants used available which are easy to use for immediate impact. These bedding plants are raised over winter in nurseries, then set out as young leafy plants when they are on the point of bursting into flower. Most then flower continuously until the autumn, bringing the garden to vibrant life with their gorgeous displays of colour.

There are bedding plants for all situations, for some are sun-lovers while others tolerate shade. Tall varieties look effective at the back of beds or staked amongst others as strategic 'dot plants' while dwarf or compact types suit exposed, windy sites or positions where formal neatness is important. Don't forget there are also many exciting foliage plants such as coleus, helichrysum or kochia, for adding leaf colour and form.

Whole beds can be laid out in a formal arrangement of plants with complementary colours, but these plants work just as well grown in groups among other garden plants, using bold patches of salvias, marigolds and antirrhinums to fill in among perennial plants and shrubs for example, or ribbons of lobelia and ageratum to edge narrow beds. Most are also perfect for growing in containers such as pots, window-boxes and hanging baskets to celebrate summer on patios and walls.

A Buyers Guide

The easiest approach to bedding is to buy seedlings for growing on or young plants ready for setting out. 'Plugs' are tiny plants mid-way between these two stages, ready for either transplanting into trays of compost or planting straight into hanging baskets. All these options are more expensive than growing your own but avoid the tricky germination stage of some bedding species.

- Fully grown plants of many popular types are available for sale from late spring onwards. Do not be tempted to buy too early – nurseries raise them in heated greenhouses and offer them for sale as soon as they reach the first-flower stage, which may be too soon for planting in your garden if there is still a risk of frost. Always wait until late spring, or until you know from experience it is safe to expose tender young plants in the outside.

- When buying, look for sturdy compact plants that have not been forced, with healthy green leaves: bare stems and yellow, wilting leaves indicate neglect, which may affect later performance.

- Plants are often in bud or bear the first open flower, but full flowering is often a sign of excessive forcing, or stress caused by drought or some other mismanagement.

- Make sure plants are clearly labelled with as much information as possible – some petunias are more weather-proof than others, for example, and a sound choice can avoid disappointment in a wet season.

- When you get your plants home, plant as soon as you can; if this is not possible, stand plants in light shade and water regularly, feeding them once or twice to keep them in good condition.

Planting

A few species flower best in poor soils but most enjoy good conditions, so prepare the ground well for a prolonged display. (The specific soil requirement for each plant is explained later.)

- The soil is best dug in autumn, adding plenty of garden compost or well-rotted manure to add humus and help retain moisture.

- Choose the right time to plant, when the soil is warming up and is still moist but not too wet.

- Make sure plants are hardened off – put them outside for a few hours each day to get used to outdoors conditions – and that severe frosts are over.

- Weed and level the surface, raking in a dressing of general fertilizer.

- Water the plants and then stand them in position, still in their pots, to check their arrangement and spacing.

- Using a trowel, dig a hole large enough to take the roots without cramping them. Lift each plant carefully from its tray or pot, and position the rootball just below the surface.

- Return the soil to the hole and firm gently with your fingers. Water each plant individually with a watering can.

Care

Watering: Regular watering is usually essential, and plants in the open ground should be watered every 7–10 days in dry weather. Either water each plant individually, or soak complete beds, but do it thoroughly, because a policy of 'little and often' encourages surface roots which are unable to fend for themselves. A 5cm (2in) mulch of garden compost or lawn mowings helps to keep the soil moist and also suppresses weeds. Containers and hanging baskets need checking daily in hot weather.

Feeding: Plants grown in beds and borders need only an occasional feed to prolong flowering – once or twice about mid- to late summer is usually enough. Plants in containers exhaust nutrients in the compost after about 6 weeks, and should then be fed every week.

Deadheading: Many bedding plants are 'self-cleaning' and voluntarily shed their faded blooms. Others will set seeds, wasting energy and interrupting flowering, and these need deadheading to maintain the display. Check over plants at regular intervals and nip or cut off the dead flowers without removing too much stem.

Raising your own bedding

Sowing outdoors
Sow outdoors in a nursery bed or where plants are to flower, in a fine seedbed prepared with a rake. Sow sparingly in rows, cover with a little soil and protect from birds. Thin seedlings when they are large enough to handle; surplus seedlings may be transplanted elsewhere if lifted carefully.

Sowing indoors
Use good quality seed compost to fill clean containers to just below the rim. Sow thinly on the surface, and cover with a thin layer of compost or leave exposed according to directions. Sow larger seeds in individual pots, or space out evenly in trays. Cover with glass or polythene until the seedlings start to emerge. Prick out when large enough to handle, about 5cm (2in) apart in trays of universal compost or individually in small pots. About 2–3 weeks before planting out, start hardening plants gradually to get them used to outdoor temperatures.

Abutilon pictum var. variegatum Flowering Maple

ABUTILON PICTUM VAR. VARIEGATUM

One of the Abutilons for summer bedding, and an outstanding foliage 'dot' plant that doubles as a handsome conservatory shrub. Flowering kinds have conspicuous bell-shaped blooms, and make fine pot or container plants.

Plant type:	Tender perennial.
Flowering time:	Early summer to early autumn; foliage types useful all year round.
Height:	60cm–1.8m (2–6ft)
Spread:	60–90cm (2–3ft)
Soil:	Light, fertile and well-drained.
Positioning:	Full sun, 60–90cm (2–3ft) apart.
Planting time:	After last frosts.
Propagation:	Take cuttings spring or summer, and plant in warmth; sow flowering kinds at 21°C (70°F) in late winter and prick out into small pots.
Care:	Pot on cuttings and seedlings into 12cm (5in) pots as they develop. Either plant outdoors in sheltered positions and stake securely, or pot on into larger containers for specimen display.
Recommended:	Variegated – *A. pictum* 'Thompsonii' and var. *variegatum*, *A. megapotamicum* 'Variegatum'; Flowering – 'Large-flowered Mixed', 'Ashford Red', 'Boule de Neige' (white), 'Canary Bird' (yellow), 'Orange Glow'.

Ageratum houstonianum Ageratum, Floss Flower

| | | |

Plant type: Half-hardy annual.

Flowering time: Early summer to mid-autumn.

Height: 15–50cm (6–20in)

Spread: 15–30cm (6–12in)

Soil: Most soils if fertile and moist.

Positioning: Full sun or light shade, 15–20cm (6–8in) apart. Use as edging to formal schemes, or for filling bare patches in borders.

Planting time: After last frosts.

Propagation: Surface-sow at 21°C (70°F) in late winter or early spring, and prick out into trays or small pots; take cuttings in spring from plants over-wintered at 10°C (50°F).

Care: Water generously in dry summers and deadhead regularly to prolong flowering until the first frosts.

Recommended: 'Adriatic', 'Blue Horizon', 'Blue Mink', 'Bavaria' (blue/white), 'Blue Bouquet' (tall for cutting), 'Capri', 'Swing Mixed'.

AGERATUM HOUSTONIANUM 'BLUE MINK'

Ageratum is a fine blue bedding plant, with neat mounds covered in bloom, especially when deadheaded and watered lavishly. There are good pink varieties but white forms brown with age. Pot some plants in late summer for window-sills. (syn. *A. mexicanum*.)

Amaranthus caudatus Love-Lies-Bleeding

AMARANTHUS CAUDATUS

The tassels on this lovely bedding highlight can reach 45cm (18in) long or more. The flowers are good for cutting and with care can be dried without loss of colour. 'Joseph's Coat' is grown for its brilliant multicoloured foliage.

Plant type: Half-hardy annual.

Flowering time: Early summer to early autumn.

Height: 30cm–1.2m (1–4ft)

Spread: 30–60cm (12–24in)

Soil: Fertile, moist but well-drained, and with a little lime.

Positioning: Full sun, 30–60cm (12–24in) apart.

Planting time: After last frosts.

Propagation: Sow at 21°C (70°F) in early spring and prick out into small pots. Harden off very carefully before planting out.

Care: Water in thoroughly after planting and do not let plants dry out in a hot season – regular watering promotes plants with fine red stems and coppery leaves in autumn. Support plants with twigs in windy positions.

Recommended: Basic species, and 'Pygmy Torch' (dwarf crimson), 'Green Thumb' (dwarf green), 'Viridis' (green); also A. paniculatus 'Red Cathedral' (tall, red foliage) and A. tricolor 'Joseph's Coat' (variegated).

Plant type: Slightly tender perennial, grown as half-hardy annual.

Flowering time: Early summer to mid-autumn.

Height: 15–90cm (6in–3ft)

Spread: 15–45cm (6–18in)

Soil: Light or medium, fertile and well-drained.

Positioning: Full sun, 15–45cm (6–18in) apart.

Planting time: Mid- to late spring.

Propagation: Sow at 18°C (65°F) in early spring and prick out into trays, or in a cold frame in early autumn; take cuttings in late summer.

Care: Either pinch out the tips of plants while still small, or remove central flower spikes as soon as blooms fade to prevent seeding and so encourage further side-blooms.

Recommended: Tall – 'Giant Forerunner', 'Madam Butterfly', 'Liberty'; Intermediate – 'Cheerio', 'Coronette', 'Monarch'; Dwarf – 'Double Sweetheart', 'Floral Carpet', 'Little Darling', 'Royal Carpet' (all mixtures; single colours also available).

ANTIRRHINUM MAJUS 'CORONETTE MIXED'

An old and lasting favourite, despite a tendency to damp off as seedlings and to contract rust late in the season. They may be grown in pots under glass for early and late flowering, and will also survive mild winters as hardy perennials.

9

Arctotis × hybrida African Daisy

ARCTOTIS × HYBRIDA 'FLAME'

South African plants with vivid flowers in succession all summer, especially in hot sunny positions. Try some as pot plants and for cutting. New hybrids offer an enormous range of colours – white, yellow, reds and blues – and pretty silvery foliage.

Plant type:	Tender perennial, grown as half-hardy annual.
Flowering time:	Mid-summer to mid-autumn.
Height:	30–90cm (1–3ft)
Spread:	30–45cm (12–18in)
Soil:	Light and well-drained, with some humus.
Positioning:	Full sun, 23cm (9in) apart.
Planting time:	After last frosts.
Propagation:	Sow at 15°C (60°F) in early spring, and prick out into small pots.
Care:	Make sure plants are fully hardened off before planting out, as they are very sensitive to frost. Pinch out growing tips while plants are still small to encourage bushiness. In wet districts grow in pots under glass, as flowers do not always open in gloomy weather. Support stems with twiggy sticks.
Recommended:	'Harlequin Hybrids', 'Large-flowered Hybrids'; also *A. acaulis* (dwarf, orange), *A. auriculata* (bright yellow) and *A. venusta* (pale blue).

Argyranthemum frutescens
Marguerite, Paris Daisy

❄ ☼

Plant type:	Tender perennial or half-hardy annual.
Flowering time:	Early summer to mid-autumn.
Height:	30–90cm (1–3ft)
Spread:	23–60cm (9–24in)
Soil:	Light, fertile and free-draining, with a little lime.
Positioning:	Full sun, 30–45cm (12–18in) apart.
Planting time:	After last frosts.
Propagation:	Sow at 15°C (60°F) in early spring and prick out into small pots; cuttings in gentle heat, in mid-spring or late summer.
Care:	Apart from watering, little attention is needed until autumn when plants are potted up and brought under cover for overwintering in the greenhouse. Keep frost-free and barely moist, and take cuttings in spring.
Recommended:	'Whity' (from seed); also 'Album Plenum' (double), 'Jamaica Primrose', 'Petite Pink', 'Qinta White', 'Rollason's Red', 'Vancouver' (pink anemone-centred).

ARGYRANTHEMUM FRUTESCENS 'JAMAICA PRIMROSE'

Once marguerites were only white, but now there are dozens of good perennial varieties in yellow, pink or red. All make neat specimen plants, or may be trained as standards, spectacular for pots and other containers. (syn. *Chrysanthemum frutescens*.).

Begonia semperflorens

BEGONIA SEMPERFLORENS

Both a house and bedding plant, free-flowering hybrids are now very popular, especially in mixtures with green, red and bronze foliage. They are tricky to raise from seed, so buy plantlets or plugs in spring, and take cuttings for overwintering.

Plant type: Tender perennial, grown as half-hardy annual.

Flowering time: Mid-summer to mid-autumn.

Height: 15–30cm (6–12in)

Spread: 15–30cm (6–12in)

Soil: Rich and moist.

Positioning: Partial shade, 15–30cm (6–12in) apart.

Planting time: After last frosts.

Propagation: Surface-sow at 21°C (70°F) in mid-winter, keep moist at all times, and prick out into trays or small pots; take cuttings of young shoots at any time.

Care: One of the best bedding plants for shade if kept watered in dry weather. Shorten long stems occasionally (prunings make good cuttings), and pot up plants in autumn for overwintering in frost-free conditions.

Recommended: 'Cocktail', 'Coco', 'Excel', 'Options' and 'Pin-up' mixtures; 'Danica Scarlet', 'Rusher Red', 'Viva' (white) and other single colours.

Begonia × tuberhybrida Tuberous Begonia

Plant type: Tender perennial tuber.

Flowering time: Early summer to early autumn.

Height: 30–45cm (12–18in), trailing to 60cm (24in)

Spread: 30–45cm (12–18in)

Soil: Rich and moist.

Positioning: Light shade, 23–30cm (9–12in) apart.

Planting time: After last frosts.

Propagation: Sow as for *B. semperflorens*; plant tubers at 21°C (70°F), hollow side uppermost and pressed into trays of moist compost; transfer to pots when growth appears.

Care: Support large-flowered varieties with twigs or canes and string, and pinch out the smaller female outer flowers beside each main bloom.

Recommended: 'Clips', 'Giant-flowered Hybrids', 'Non-stop', 'Pin-Up' and 'Show Angels' mixtures, and many named varieties; also *B. hortensis* 'All Round Mixed' (trailing); *B. multiflora* (numerous smaller blooms); *B. pendula* (trailing) 'Chanson', 'Happy End' and 'Illumination'.

BEGONIA × TUBERHYBRIDA

Flamboyant and dazzling, with enormous flowers in white, yellow, pink and red, often edged or marked with contrasting shades. Keep well-watered, and when flowering finishes remove the stems and dry tubers for storing over winter.

Brachycome iberidifolia Swan River Daisy

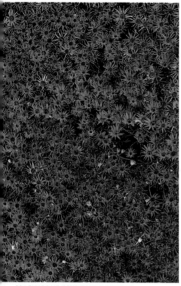

BRACHYCOME IBERIDIFOLIA 'BLUE STAR'

An Australian plant with ferny leaves and sweetly fragrant blooms in white, pink, blue or purple. Some forms are neat and compact for edging, while others sprawl lazily and need support or can be used in hanging baskets.

Plant type:	Half-hardy or hardy annual.
Flowering time:	Early summer to early autumn.
Height:	23–30cm (9–12in)
Spread:	15–23cm (6–9in)
Soil:	Light, rich and free-draining.
Positioning:	Full sun or light shade, 23cm (9in) apart.
Planting time:	Late spring.
Propagation:	Sow at 13°C (55°F) in early spring and prick out into trays; pinch the tips of seedlings for bushy growth.
Care:	Make sure plants are sheltered from the wind, and water well in dry weather to promote flowering. In a hot season plants may finish flowering early, and it is a good idea to sow a further batch in late spring for continuity – these plants may be potted up to flower under glass if not needed for bedding.
Recommended:	Normal species mixture; also 'Blue Gleam', 'Blue Star', 'Brachy Blue', 'Purple Splendour', 'Violet Splendour', 'White Splendour'.

Calceolaria rugosa Slipper Flower

Plant type:	Tender perennial, grown as half-hardy annual.
Flowering time:	Early summer to mid-autumn.
Height:	20–45cm (8–18in)
Spread:	20–30cm (8–12in)
Soil:	Any kind if moist and fertile.
Positioning:	Full sun or light shade, 23cm (9in) apart.
Planting time:	Late spring or early summer.
Propagation:	Surface-sow at 21°C (70°F) in late winter, prick out into trays, then transfer to individual pots and grow at a cool temperature; take cuttings in autumn.
Care:	Plants are normally very reliable, but they benefit from a good soak in hot weather. Dig up a few before the first frosts, and pot or pack together in a deep seedbox for overwintering under frost-free glass. Keep just moist, then revive plants again in spring for cuttings.
Recommended:	'Golden Bunch', 'Midas', 'Sunshine'; also *C. biflora*, basic species or 'Goldcrest'.

CALCEOLARIA RUGOSA 'SUNSHINE'

Not the multicoloured glasshouse Calceolarias, but a traditional Victorian favourite, making neat woody plants smothered with yellow or gold pouches. Not easy to raise from seed, but bought plants can be perpetuated from cuttings.

Calendula officinalis Pot Marigold, English Marigold

CALENDULA OFFICINALIS 'FIESTA GITANA'

A popular cottage garden flower and ornamental herb, available in various shades of yellow, orange, cream and brown. Excellent for cutting and can also be dried for use as a substitute for saffron. Self-sown plants pop up charmingly in nooks and crannies around the garden.

Plant type: Hardy annual.

Flowering time: Late spring until the first frosts (in a very mild season rarely out of flower).

Height: 23–60cm (9–24in)

Spread: 23–30cm (9–12in)

Soil: Most kinds if moist and fairly fertile.

Positioning: Full sun or light shade, 23cm (9in) apart in patches in beds.

Planting time: Mid- or late spring; also mid-autumn.

Propagation: Sow in frost-free conditions under glass in late winter and prick out into trays, or sow outdoors in situ in early spring; may also be sown in autumn, either in situ or in trays for pricking out, and these will flower early the following spring. Plants self-seed freely.

Care: Water spring transplants, especially in a dry season. Deadhead regularly for a long display.

Recommended: Normal species, and also 'Art Shades', 'Fiesta Gitana', 'Golden Princess', 'Orange King', 'Pacific Beauty', 'Radio' and 'Sunglow'.

Callistephus chinensis China Aster, Annual Aster

Plant type: Hardy/half-hardy annual.
Flowering time: Late summer to mid-autumn.
Height: 15–90cm (6in–3ft)
Spread: 23–45cm (9–18in)
Soil: Fertile and well-drained, with a little lime.
Positioning: Full sun with shelter from winds, 23–45cm (9–18in) apart.
Planting time: Late spring.
Propagation: Sow at 10–15°C (50–60°F) in early spring, and prick out into small pots or in a cold frame 5cm (2in) apart.
Care: Do not grow in the same place in two consecutive seasons as serious fungal diseases can build up.
Recommended: Tall – 'Duchess Mixed', 'Giant Princess', 'Giant Single Andrella', 'Super Sinensis'; Medium – 'Early Ostrich Plume', 'Gusford Supreme', 'Pompon Mixed'; Dwarf – 'Carpet Ball', 'Colour Carpet', 'Crimson Sunset', 'Lilliput', 'Milady'.

CALLISTEPHUS CHENENSIS

Generally known as asters, the enormous choice of *Callistephus* varieties provides a supreme source of late summer colour just when other plants are past their best. The whole spectrum of shades is available as single or double blooms.

Canna hybrida Indian Shot

CANNA HYBRIDA 'ASSAULT'

An exotic 'dot' plant, adding a tropical touch to summer bedding. Canna flowers are up to 15cm (6in) across, in a number of bright or sultry shades, while the lush leaves are green, bronze or purple. Dig up in autumn and store like dahlias. (syn. *C. generalis*, *C. indica*.)

Plant type: Tender perennial.

Flowering time: Mid-summer to mid-autumn.

Height: 60cm–1.2m (2–4ft)

Spread: 60cm (2ft)

Soil: Rich and moist.

Positioning: Full sun, 45–60cm (18–24in) apart.

Planting time: After last frosts.

Propagation: Chip seeds and soak in tepid water for 24hrs, then sow singly in pots at 21°C (70°F) in late winter; divide mature rhizomes in early spring and start growing in pots at 15°C (60°F).

Care: Feed every week or so as they are greedy plants, and water regularly in dry summers. Bring indoors before first frosts and pot or box up until they die down naturally, then cut the dead leaves and roots from the rhizomes before storing.

Recommended: Basic species, and many named varieties, such as 'Assault', 'Black Knight', 'Golden Lucifer', 'Orchid', 'Picasso', 'President', 'Purpurea' and 'Tropical Rose'.

Plant type: Half-hardy annual.

Flowering time: Mid-summer to mid-autumn.

Height: 10cm–1.2m (4in–4ft)

Spread: 10–45cm (4–18in)

Soil: Light, fertile and well-drained.

Positioning: Full sun with shelter from winds, 10–30cm (4–12in) apart.

Planting time: Plant after last frosts.

Propagation: Sow at 21°C (70°F) in early spring and prick out into small pots; keep warm and pot on as required. Harden off very thoroughly before planting out.

Care: Varieties are very tender, and must be well hardened off before planting out. If you cannot provide shelter and very free drainage, grow instead as a container plant in soil-based compost.

Recommended: Tall – 'Century Mixed', 'Flamingo Feather', 'Pampas Plume'; Dwarf – 'Dwarf Geisha', 'Fairy Fountains' and 'Lilliput'; also C. cristata (Cockscomb) 'Coral Garden Mixed' or 'Jewel Box Mixed'.

CELOSIA ARGENTEA PLUMOSA GROUP

In a sunny sheltered spot, this pot plant is equally happy as a bedding 'dot' plant, while taller varieties are excellent for cutting and drying. C. cristata has tightly packed flowers in a crest 15–30cm (6–12in) wide, and is used for the same purposes. syn. C. plumosa.)

CENTAUREA CYANUS

The native wild blue cornflower has been transformed into a valuable bedding plant and cut flower, in colours from white to deep red and purple. Closely related sweet sultan has powder-puff flowers in a similarly wide colour choice. Deadhead both kinds regularly.

Plant type:	Hardy annual.
Flowering time:	Early summer to mid-autumn.
Height:	20–90cm (8in–3ft)
Spread:	20–30cm (8–12in)
Soil:	Light, fairly rich and well-drained, with a little lime.
Positioning:	Full sun, 23–30cm (9–12in) apart.
Planting time:	Late spring.
Propagation:	Sow in a cold frame in early spring or early autumn, or outdoors in mid-spring where plants are to grow. May also be sown in situ in autumn to produce larger, stronger plants that flower a little earlier than transplants.
Care:	In windy gardens support the wiry stems with twigs, or grow plants between other sturdier kinds.
Recommended:	'Black Ball', 'Blue Diadem', 'Frosty Mixed', 'Jubilee Gem', 'Polka Dot Mixed', 'Snowman'; also *C. moschata* (Sweet Sultan) 'Dairy Maid', 'Imperialis Mixed', 'The Bride'.

Plant type: Hardy/half-hardy annual.

Flowering time: Early summer to mid-autumn.

Height: 10–90cm (4in–3ft)

Spread: 23–45cm (9–18in)

Soil: Light, fertile and well-drained, with lime.

Positioning: Full sun, 15–30cm (6–12in) apart.

Planting time: Late spring.

Propagation: Sow in a cold frame in early spring, or outdoors in mid-spring where plants are to flower. May also be sown in autumn for earlier blooms.

Care: Water well in dry weather and support taller varieties with twiggy sticks. Watch out for greenfly and spray with a systemic insecticide at the first signs.

Recommended: 'Court Jesters Mixed', 'Merry Mixture', 'Polar Star', 'Rainbow Mixture', 'Tricolor Mixed'; also C. coronarium (Crown Daisy) 'Golden Gem', 'Primrose Gem'; C. multicaule 'Gold Plate', 'Moonlight'.

CHRYSANTHEMUM CARINATUM VARIETY

One of the most cheerful and traditional of bedding plants, dependable in most seasons, especially if deadheaded. There are varieties for all purposes, from neat dwarf edging to long-lasting cut flowers; spreading C. multicaule is ideal for baskets. (syn. C. tricolor.)

Clarkia unguiculata Clarkia, Farewell to Spring

CLARKIA UNGUICULATA 'ROYAL BOUQUET'

An old Victorian favourite, showy and easy to grow. The double flowers are extravagantly frilled, like double hollyhocks. *C. pulchella* is slender and shorter, with dainty semi-double flowers, while *C. concinna* (Red Ribbons) is a pretty pink Californian species. (syn. *C. elegans*.)

✳✳

Plant type: Hardy annual.

Flowering time: Mid-summer to early autumn.

Height: 30–75cm (12–30in)

Spread: 23–30cm (9–12in)

Soil: Light, rich, slightly acid.

Positioning: Full sun or light shade, 23cm (9in) apart, in patches in beds and borders.

Planting time: Mid-spring.

Propagation: Sow in situ, in mid- or late spring and early summer for succession; also in early autumn under glass for earlier flowering.

Care: Best sown in situ but autumn sowings may be pricked out into small pots for spring transplanting with minimal root disturbance; overwinter seedlings in a cold frame. Pinch out growing tips for bushy growth, and support taller varieties with twiggy sticks. Do not over-water.

Recommended: Normal species mixed, and 'Apple Blossom', 'Chieftan', 'Royal Bouquet Mixed' and 'Salmon Queen'.

Plant type: Half-hardy annual.

Flowering time: Early summer to mid-autumn

Height: 90cm–1.2m (3–4ft)

Spread: 45–60cm (18–24in)

Soil: Light, fertile and well-drained.

Positioning: Full sun with shelter from wind, 45–60cm (18–24in) apart.

Planting time: Late spring.

Propagation: Sow at 21°C (70°F) in late winter and early spring, pricking out into individual pots.

Care: Cold winds are lethal at any time, but especially while plants are young, so make sure they are fully hardened off before planting out. Check regularly for greenfly and treat this with systemic insecticide.

Recommended: Normal species mixed and 'Colour Fountain Mixed'; also separate colours such as 'Cherry Queen', 'Helen Campbell' (white), 'Pink Queen' and 'Violet Queen'.

CLEOME SPINOSA 'COLOUR FOUNTAIN'

A dramatic and exotic choice for a large 'dot' plant or bold group in a border, or as a summer hedge. The spidery flowers reach 8cm (3in) or more in length and then form curious seedpods. Shelter from wind is important, and generous watering in dry weather. (syn. *C. hassleriana*.)

Coleus blumei Flame Nettle

COLEUS BLUMEI VARIETY

There are two main kinds of Coleus: named varieties grown under glass and propagated by cuttings only, and the various mixtures or separate colours listed here and used as pot plants or foliage bedding plants in a range of extravagant colours. (syn. *Solenostemon scutellarioides*.)

Plant type:	Tender perennial, grown as half-hardy annual.
Flowering time:	Foliage plant, flowers insignificant.
Height:	15–45cm (6–18in)
Spread:	15–45cm (6–18in)
Soil:	Light and dryish or well-drained.
Positioning:	Full sun or light shade, 15–30cm (6–12in) apart.
Planting time:	After last frosts.
Propagation:	Surface-sow at 21°C (70°F) in late winter or early spring, and prick out into small pots; take stem cuttings in early spring.
Care:	Pinch out tips occasionally to induce bushy growth, and remove any flower buds as they form to prevent early leaf loss. Pot up in autumn and keep just moist under frost-free glass for cuttings the following spring.
Recommended:	'Rainbow Mixture', 'Sabre Mixed', 'Wizard Mixed'; also 'Red Velvet', 'Salmon Lace', 'Scarlet Poncho' (trailing), and 'Volcano' (scarlet).

Convolvulus tricolor Dwarf Morning Glory

Plant type: Hardy annual.
Flowering time: Mid-summer to mid-autumn.
Height: 15–38cm (6–15in)
Spread: Up to 50cm (20in)
Soil: Light, poor and well-drained.
Positioning: Full sun, 23cm (9in) apart.
Planting time: Late spring.
Propagation: Pre-soak seeds for 24 hours before sowing in small pots at 10°C (50°F) in early spring, or outdoors in mid-spring where plants are to grow.
Care: Plant out while still small as larger plants do not establish easily, especially in a hot dry season.
Recommended: 'Choice Mixed', 'Dwarf Rainbow Flash Mixed'; also separates 'Blue Ensign', 'Rose Ensign', 'Royal Ensign' (deep blue and gold) and 'White Ensign'.

CONVOLVULUS TRICOLOR

This makes bushy plants smothered in beautiful 5cm (2in) trumpets, each lasting for only a day but the overall display continues all summer, especially if plants are deadheaded occasionally. An ideal choice for sunny, dry or impoverished sites. (syn. *C. minor*.)

COREOPSIS TINCTORIA 'DWARF DAZZLER'

One of the most vivid annuals, like a large French marigold, in exciting shades of yellow, red and brown. Varieties such as 'Dwarf Dazzler' are neat and ideal for the front of the border or containers, while taller kinds are excellent for cutting. (syn. *Calliopsis bicolor*.)

Plant type: Hardy/half-hardy annual.

Flowering time: Mid-summer to early autumn.

Height: 30–90cm (1–3ft)

Spread: 23–38cm (9–15in)

Soil: Light, fertile and well-drained.

Positioning: Full sun, 23–30cm (9–12in) apart.

Planting time: Late spring.

Propagation: Sow at 18°C (65°F) in early spring, or in mid-spring outdoors where plants are to flower.

Care: Full recommended spacings stimulate bushy growth. Stake tall varieties and deadhead regularly.

Recommended: 'Dwarf Dazzler', 'Dwarf Delight', 'Dwarf Mixed', 'Fiery Beam' (bronze-red, dwarf), 'Tall Mixed'; also *C. drummondii* (syn. *C. basalis*) 'Golden Crown' and 'Golden King', and *C. stillmanii* 'Golden Fleece'.

	Plant type:	Half-hardy annual.
	Flowering time:	Mid-summer until first frosts.
	Height:	30–90cm (1–3ft)
	Spread:	30–45cm (12–18in)
	Soil:	Light, fertile and well-drained.
	Positioning:	Full sun, 30–45cm (12–18in) apart.
	Planting time:	Late spring or early summer.
	Propagation:	Sow at 10°C (50°F) in early or mid-spring and prick out into small pots.
	Care:	Young plants can be very tender, so harden off well before planting out. Taller plants may need holding up with pea sticks unless grown in mutually self-supporting groups. Deadhead faded blooms occasionally.
	Recommended:	'Candy Stripe', 'Daydream Mixed', 'Dazzler' (crimson), 'Early Sensation', 'Psyche Mixed', 'Purity' (white), 'Sensation', 'Sonata'; also C. sulphureus 'Ladybird Mixed', 'Sunny Gold', 'Sunny Orange-red', 'Sunset'.

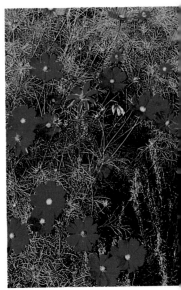

COSMOS BIPINNATUS 'SENSATION'

Many *Cosmos* varieties are tall and well suited for filling gaps in borders or as bold centrepieces within bedding schemes. Most are pink, white or red, but Klondyke Cosmos (*C. sulphureus*) varieties add scarlet and vivid yellows to the range.

Dahlia hybrids Dahlia

DAHLIA HYBRIDS 'BISHOP OF LLANDAFF'

Bedding dahlias are dwarf versions of tall border varieties, with a similar range of colour and flower form. Regular watering and feeding ensures a long flowering season, after which tubers may be lifted for storing and replanting the next year.

Plant type: Tender perennial, grown as half-hardy annual.

Flowering time: Mid-summer to first frosts.

Height: 30–60cm (12–24in)

Spread: 30–45cm (12–18in)

Soil: Rich and moisture-retentive, with plenty of humus.

Positioning: Full sun, 30cm (12in) apart.

Planting time: Tubers mid-spring; growing plants after last frosts.

Propagation: Sow at 18°C (65°F) in late winter and early spring, and prick out into individual pots; divide tubers in spring before planting; take cuttings in late spring.

Care: Deadhead regularly. Wait until frost has blackened whole plant before digging up tubers. Cut off stems and stand tubers upside-down to dry for a week or so. Scrape off all soil and store in dry frost-free conditions.

Recommended: 'Coltness Hybrids', 'Dandy' (collarette), 'Diablo', 'Figaro', 'Redskin', 'Rigoletto' and 'Sunny Yellow'.

Delphinium consolida
Larkspur, Annual Delphinium

**

Plant type:	Hardy annual.
Flowering time:	Early summer to early autumn.
Height:	30cm–1.2m (1–4ft)
Spread:	30–45cm (12–18in)
Soil:	Fertile and well-drained.
Positioning:	Full sun or light shade with shelter from winds, 30cm (12in) apart.
Planting time:	Late spring.
Propagation:	Sow at 13°C (55°F) in early spring and prick out into small pots; for a long season sow in situ in early autumn and again in mid-spring.
Care:	Best sown in situ and thinned in showery weather so that thinnings may be tansplanted immediately. In hot dry gardens grow in light shade and water regularly to prolong flowering.
Recommended:	'Dwarf Hyacinth-flowered Mixed', 'Frosted Skies', 'Giant Imperial Mixed', 'Giant Imperial White', 'Imperial White King' and 'Sublime Mixed'.

DELPHINIUM CONSOLIDA 'GIANT IMPERIAL WHITE'

A lovely and graceful cottage garden favourite, with a relatively short season in hot summers. The flower spikes are perfect for cutting, and many modern forms have been developed for this purpose, including a number of separate colour lines. (syn *D. ajacis, Consolida ambigua*.)

DIANTHUS CHINENSIS 'SNOWFIRE'

Brilliant and colourful 'annual' pinks that are in fact perennials, easily kept from one year to the next in cool well-drained conditions. Water regularly and deadhead for a continuous sea of colour from blooms that may be 5cm (2in) across and intricately marked.

Plant type: Tender perennial, grown as half-hardy annual.

Flowering time: Early summer to mid-autumn.

Height: 15–30cm (6–12in)

Spread: 15–30cm (6–12in)

Soil: Light, fertile and well-drained, with lime.

Positioning: Full sun or light shade, 15cm (6in) apart.

Planting time: Late spring or early summer.

Propagation: Sow at 10°C (50°F) in early spring, prick out into small pots and grow on in cool conditions; divide overwintered plants in spring.

Care: As plants are short-lived perennials, try digging some up before flowering ceases and pack into seed boxes filled with soil-based compost. Keep just moist all winter, and divide or take cuttings in spring.

Recommended: 'Fire Carpet', 'Magic Charms Mixed', 'Princess Mixed', 'Raspberry Parfait', 'Snowfire', 'Telstar Mixed'.

Dimorphotheca aurantiaca Star of the Veldt

DIMORPHOTHECA AURANTIACA

Plant type: Tender perennial, grown as half-hardy annual.

Flowering time: Early summer to early autumn.

Height: 20–45cm (8–18in)

Spread: 30–38cm (12–15in)

Soil: Fertile and very well-drained.

Positioning: Sunniest possible, 30cm (12in) apart.

Planting time: Late spring or early summer.

Propagation: Sow at 15°C (60°F) in early spring and prick out into small pots; take cuttings in autumn, and grow on in cool conditions.

Care: For maximum floral impact, do not water or feed too often. Plants may be lifted in autumn and overwintered under glass, minimum temperature 7°C (45°F). Water very sparingly until spring.

Recommended: 'Aurantiaca Hybrids', 'Glistening White', 'Salmon Queen', 'Tetra Pole Star'; also many named varieties such as 'Buttermilk', 'Pink Whirls', 'Silver Sparkler' and 'Whirligig'.

There is great confusion between various Dimorphotheca and Osteospermum varieties, some grown from seed and others bought as named plants. All produce mats of sun-loving blooms, 5cm (2in) across) in many colours, that often shine or sparkle in the sunlight. (syn. *Osteospermum hybrida*.)

Dorotheanthus bellidiformis Livingstone Daisy

DOREANTHUS BELLIDIFORMIS 'GELATTO DARK PINK'

A spreading annual that thrives in the hottest, sunniest positions, producing glistening carpets of wide brilliant daisies in a mixture of apricot, pink, orange and red. These tend to close in dull weather, although yellow 'Lunette' is less fussy. (syn. *Mesembryanthemum criniflorum*.)

Plant type: Half-hardy annual.

Flowering time: Early summer to early autumn.

Height: 8–15cm (3–6in)

Spread: 15–20cm (6–8in)

Soil: Very light, and dry or well-drained.

Positioning: Full sun, 20cm (8in) apart.

Planting time: After last frosts.

Propagation: Sow at 15°C (60°F) in early spring and prick out into small pots.

Care: Young plants are very tender and should be fully hardened off before planting out. Protect them against slugs, which are attracted to the plants, and deadhead regularly.

Recommended: Basic species mixture, and 'Magic Carpet Mixed', 'Gelatto Dark Pink', 'Gelatto White'; also *D. oculatus* (syn. *Mesembryanthemum oculatus*), 'Lunette' (syn. 'Yellow Ice'), yellow/red eye.

Echium plantagineum Viper's Bugloss

| ** | ▦ | ▢ | ♓ |

Plant type: Hardy annual/biennial.

Flowering time: Early summer to mid-autumn.

Height: 30–90cm (1–3ft).

Spread: 15–45cm (6–18in)

Soil: Light, fertile and well-drained.

Positioning: Full sun, 23–30cm (9–12in) apart.

Planting time: Late spring.

Propagation: Sow in a cold frame in early spring and prick out into small pots; or sow in situ, in late summer or mid-spring.

Care: All echiums are popular with bees and can be planted near hives or in the kitchen garden to attract pollinators. There is no need to water unless the season is very dry, and support is only necessary in exposed gardens.

Recommended: Basic species; also dwarf hybrids such as 'Blue Ball', 'Blue Bedder', 'Dwarf Hybrids', 'Mixed Bedder'.

ECHIUM PLANTAGINEUM 'BLUE BALL'

The basic species is tall with deep blue flowers, ideal for mixed borders. Garden varieties have extended the colour range to include pinks, reds and white, and are all short drought-tolerant bedding plants with fragrant bell-shaped blooms. (syn. *E. vulgare*.)

33

Eschscholzia californica — Californian Poppy

ESCHSCHOLZIA CALIFORNICA

A charming annual that revels in poor soils. Dainty, finely cut foliage and silky blooms in a stunning range of colours make this a desirable bedder, best sown in situ as it resents transplanting. Self-set seedlings pop up in surprising places.

Plant type: Hardy annual.

Flowering time: Early summer to early autumn.

Height: 15–38cm (6–15in)

Spread: 15cm (6in)

Soil: Light, poor and very well-drained.

Positioning: Full sun, 15cm (6in) apart.

Planting time: Late spring.

Propagation: Sow in situ in mid-spring; may also be sown at 15°C (60°F) in early spring, and pricked out into small pots.

Care: Deadhead regularly to prolong flowering, and make a second sowing in summer for later plants, some of which may survive the winter and flower early the following spring. Watch where self-sown plants thrive and sow more there, as these will be their preferred positions.

Recommended: 'Alba', 'Ballerina Mixed', 'Dalli' (scarlet), 'Mission Bells Mixed', 'Monarch Mixed', 'Purple Gleam', 'Red Chief', 'Thai Silk Series'; also E. caespitosa 'Sundew' (yellow, squarish blooms).

Felicia ameloides Kingfisher Daisy, Blue Marguerite

FELICIA AMELOIDES

| | | |

Plant type: Tender perennial or half-hardy annual.

Flowering time: Mid-summer to early autumn.

Height: 15–45cm (6–18in)

Spread: 15–30cm (6–12in)

Soil: Any kind if fertile and well-drained.

Positioning: Full sun, 23cm (9in) apart.

Planting time: After last frosts.

Propagation: Sow at 15°C (60°F) in early spring and prick out into trays or small pots; take cuttings and plant in warmth, in early spring or mid-summer.

Care: Plants perform best if deadheaded and watered regularly. Either dig up plants in autumn, or take mid-summer cuttings to overwinter indoors as house plants that will start flowering early the following spring.

Recommended: Basic species or 'Cub Scout'; also *F. amelloides* (syn. *F. capensis*) in many blue, white and variegated named forms, and *F. heterophylla* 'The Blues' and 'The Rose'.

Once known as Agathea, there are several species with cultivated forms, all with bright foliage and pretty daisies in a range of attractive blues. Despite their delicate appearance, plants are robust and make a fine choice for pots and containers indoors and out.

Fuchsia hybrids Fuchsia

FUCHSIA HYBRIDS 'HERALD'

Bedding fuchsias tend to be compact and bushy, although many can be trained as standards up to 1.2m (4ft) high for dramatic 'dot' and container specimens. A few seed strains are available and, like named cultivars, these can be kept over winter for cuttings.

Plant type:	Tender perennial shrub.
Flowering time:	Mid-summer to early autumn.
Height:	30–60cm (12–24in)
Spread:	30–45cm (12–18in)
Soil:	Fertile, moist but well-drained.
Positioning:	Full sun or light shade, 45cm (18in) apart.
Planting time:	Late spring or early summer.
Propagation:	Surface-sow at 21°C (70°F) in late winter or early spring, and prick out into small pots; take soft cuttings in spring or summer.
Care:	Regular watering in dry weather is critical for keeping plants in continuous flower. Feed fuchsias in containers every week, and other plants fortnightly.
Recommended:	(Seeds) 'Chimes Mixed', 'Mixed Hybrids', 'Florabelle'; hundreds of named cultivars including 'Autumnale', 'Avocet', 'Alice Hoffman', 'Marinka', 'Mission Bells', 'Rufus the Red', 'Swingtime' and 'Golden Swingtime', 'Thalia'.

Gaillardia pulchella Blanket Flower

GAILLARDIA PULCHELLA 'LOLLIPOPS'

Plant type: Half-hardy annual.

Flowering time: Mid-summer to first frosts.

Height: 30–60cm (12–24in)

Spread: 30–45cm (12–18in)

Soil: Any fertile, well-drained soil.

Positioning: Full sun or very light shade, 23–30cm (9–12in) apart.

Planting time: After last frosts.

Propagation: Sow at 21°C (70°F) in early spring and prick out into small pots.

Care: As they are tough and tolerant of drought, these plants need little special care. Perennial varieties can be kept from one year to the next if you take cuttings in late summer for overwintering in a cold frame.

Recommended: 'Double Mixed', 'Gaiety Mixed', 'Lollipops' syn. *G. p.* var. *lorenziana* (double, quilled petals), 'Red Plume'; also *G. aristata* (tender or hardy perennial), 'Goblin' (red/yellow) and 'Golden Goblin', 'Torchlight' (tall).

A beautiful plant with large flowers 8–10cm (3–4in) across in rich combinations of red, yellow, pink and purple. Dwarf kinds are best for bedding, taller varieties for cutting if deadheaded and supported with a few twigs.

GAZANIA HYBRID 'CHANSONETTE'

A gorgeous bedder that tolerates spartan conditions and is disappointing only in heavy soil or dull weather. The exotic blooms can reach 12cm (5in) across, and are particularly eye-catching with their contrasting stripes or rings of colour.

Plant type:	Tender perennial, grown as half-hardy annual.
Flowering time:	Mid-summer to first frosts.
Height:	20–45cm (8–18in)
Spread:	20–30cm (8–12in)
Soil:	Light, and dry or very well-drained.
Positioning:	Hot dry spots in full sun, 30cm (12in) apart.
Planting time:	After last frosts.
Propagation:	Sow at 18°C (65°F) in early spring and prick out into small pots; also take basal cuttings in late summer and keep frost-free over winter.
Care:	Undemanding. You can keep plants from year to year by potting them up before the first frosts for overwintering in a dry, warm place.
Recommended:	'Harlequin Hybrids', 'Chansonette', 'Mini-Star Mixed' and 'Mini-Star White', 'Sundance Mixed', 'Sunshine Mixed' and 'Talent Mixed'.

Godetia grandiflora Godetia

Plant type: Hardy annual.
Flowering time: Early summer to early autumn.
Height: 23–60cm (9–24in)
Spread: 15–45cm (6–18in)
Soil: Any fairly fertile and moisture-retentive soil.
Positioning: Full sun or very light shade, 23–30cm (9–12in) apart.
Planting time: Late spring.
Propagation: Sow in trays in a cold frame in early spring and prick out into small pots; sow in situ in early autumn and again in mid-spring for a longer season.
Care: Do not over-feed as this stimulates leaf growth at the expense of flowers. Autumn-sown seedlings may be potted up for winter flowering indoors.
Recommended: 'Bornita Mixed', 'Azalea-flowered Mixed', 'Duchess of Albany' (white), 'Dwarf Monarch Mixed', 'Firelight', 'Grace Mixed', 'Rosy Morn', 'Satin Mixed', 'Sybil Sherwood' (pink/white); also G. bottae 'Lady in Blue' and 'Lilac Blossom'.

GODETIA GRANDIFLORA 'AZALEA-FLOWERED MIXED'

An old cottage garden flower that has been improved considerably, with both dwarf and tall selections, many with attractively marked petals. Easily raised by simply scattering seeds wherever there is space, but remember to water and deadhead regularly. (syn. Clarkia rubicunda.)

Gypsophila elegans Baby's Breath

GYPSOPHILA ELEGANS

This is the elegant annual used widely by florists and flower arrangers. Outdoors it combines well with large-flowered bedding plants, but also succeeds in drifts and patches in mixed borders, trailing from walls and baskets, and as an unusual pot plant.

Plant type: Hardy annual.

Flowering time: Early summer to mid-autumn.

Height: 30–60cm (12–24in).

Spread: 30–45cm (12–18in).

Soil: Fertile, well-drained with a little lime.

Positioning: Full sun, 15cm (6in) apart.

Planting time: Normally sown in situ.

Propagation: Sow in situ in early autumn and again in mid-spring. In some seasons the flowering duration may be curtailed and it is advisable to make further sowings in early summer to ensure continuity through to autumn frosts.

Care: Plants have fairly weak, slender stems, so support with twiggy sticks is recommended. Do not feed or over-water as this produces soft sprawling growth.

Recommended: 'Covent Garden', 'Deep Rose', 'Giant White', 'Kermesina' (red), 'Monarch Mixed'.

Helianthus annuus Sunflower

Plant type: Hardy annual.
Flowering time: Early summer to mid-autumn.
Height: 60cm–3m (2–10ft) or more
Spread: 30cm–1.5m (1–5ft)
Soil: Any well-cultivated soil.
Positioning: Full sun, 30–90cm (1–3ft) apart.
Planting time: Late spring.
Propagation: Sow at 15°C (60°F) in small pots in early spring, or in mid-spring in situ.
Care: Compact bushy varieties need little feeding and only occasional watering in very dry seasons. Taller kinds, especially when grown to maximum size, benefit from feeding every week. Support with strong stakes driven firmly into the ground.
Recommended: 'Autumn Beauty', 'Holiday', 'Music Box', 'Orange Sun', 'Sonja', 'Sunburst Mixed', 'Sungold', 'Sunspot', 'Teddy Bear', 'Velvet Queen'.

HELIANTHUS ANNUUS 'SUNSPOT'

Whereas the sunflower was once a coarse giant plant with enormous yellow flowers 30cm (12in) across, there is now a whole range of yellow, orange, red and brown-flowered varieties, many bushy and branching, and some with small furry flowers like African marigolds.

41

Helichrysum bracteatum Straw Flower

HELICHRYSUM BRACTEATUM 'BIKINI'

A flower arranger's favourite in a full range of sizes, from tall plants for cutting to dwarf bushy kinds that make excellent edging. The crisp papery flowers cover the whole spectrum from white to purple, and dry well if cut just before fully open.

Plant type: Half-hardy annual.

Flowering time: Mid-summer to mid-autumn.

Height: 30cm–1.2m (1–4ft)

Spread: 15–30cm (6–12in)

Soil: Fertile and well-drained.

Positioning: Full sun, 15cm (6in) apart.

Planting time: Late spring.

Propagation: Sow at 18°C (65°F) in early spring and prick out into trays, or in situ in mid-spring.

Care: Tall varieties need support with pea sticks or canes and string. Although plants are attractive in bloom as bedding plants, start cutting some flowers for drying as soon as they open – later blooms may be imperfect in a dull or wet summer.

Recommended: Basic species, as mixtures or separate colours; also 'Bikini Mixed' and single colours, 'Frosted Sulphur', 'Pastel Mixed'; and *H. petiolatum*, non-flowering edging plant with grey felted leaves.

Heliotropium peruvianum Heliotrope, Cherry Pie

✿✿ 🏆

Plant type:	Tender perennial, grown as half-hardy annual.
Flowering time:	Early summer to early autumn.
Height:	30–75cm (12–30in)
Spread:	30–45cm (12–18in)
Soil:	Any kind if fertile and well-drained.
Positioning:	Full sun, 30cm (12in) apart.
Planting time:	After last frosts.
Propagation:	Sow at 18°C (65°F) in late winter and prick out into small pots; take cuttings from overwintered plants in spring.
Care:	Undemanding if watered in very dry weather. Dig up plants in early autum, for overwintering in pots under glass. Cuttings grown as straight single stems may be tied to canes for training up to 60cm (2ft) high before pinching out growing tips to produce standard plants.
Recommended:	Species as seed mixtures, 'Dwarf Marine' and 'Marine'; also cultivars such as 'Lord Roberts' (dark blue) and 'White Lady'.

HELIOTROPIUM PERUVIANUM 'MARINE'

An old-fashioned shrub, once grown as standards for 'dot' plants and indoor decoration, that is becoming popular again for the heady fragrance of its 15cm (6in) flower heads that rival Buddleias in their attraction for butterflies.
(syn. *H. arborescens*.)

HIBISCUS HYBRIDUS 'DIXIBELLE'

Spectacular plants for warm sites, with large conspicuous blooms, up to 23cm (9in) across in 'Dixie Belle', that individually last for only a day. Many others follow, and at the end of the season most Hibiscus can be brought inside to survive the winter.

Plant type: Tender perennials and half-hardy annuals.

Flowering time: Early summer to mid-autumn.

Height: 30–90cm (1–3ft)

Spread: 30–45cm (12–18in)

Soil: Fertile and well-drained.

Positioning: Full sun, 30cm (12in) apart.

Planting time: After last frosts.

Propagation: Soak seeds for 1 hour in hot water, sow at 24°C (75°F) in late winter and prick out into small pots; take soft cuttings in spring or summer.

Care: Feed every fortnight and water in very dry weather. Taller varieties may need staking. Pot up the best plants in autumn and keep frost-free over winter for spring cuttings.

Recommended: 'Cream Cup', 'Dixie Belle', 'Disco Belle Mixed'; also *H. rosa-sinensis*, tender perennial shrub with many named forms, and *H. trionum* (Annual Hibiscus) 'Simply Love' (yellow/brown), 'Sunny Day'.

Iberis umbellata Candytuft

** 🔲

Plant type:	Hardy annual.
Flowering time:	Late spring to mid-autumn.
Height:	20–45cm (8–18in)
Spread:	15–60cm (6–24in)
Soil:	Any well-drained soil.
Positioning:	Full sun, 10–15cm (4–6in) apart.
Planting time:	Normally sown in situ.
Propagation:	Sow in situ in early autumn and early or mid-spring.
Care:	Plants are very reliable and need little special care. In a good summer there is a danger they will flower themselves to exhaustion, so trim off the first main flush of blooms as they fade to induce more, or sow again in early summer for late succession. Protect seedlings against slugs.
Recommended:	'Dwarf Fairy(land) Mixed', 'Flash Mixed'; also *I. coronaria* (Hyacinth-flowered Candytuft) 'Iceberg' and 'White Pinnacle', and *I. crenata* (white).

IBERIS UMBELLATA

One of the easiest annuals, Iberis flowers quickly from seed which can be scattered wherever there is room – try sowing over spring bulbs to follow them as their leaves die down. Deadheading will prolong the display of blooms, fragrant and clustered together in tight domes.

Impatiens walleriana Busy Lizzie

IMPATIENS WALLERIANA SUPER ELFIN SERIES

Available in a wide range of colours, and also as double, bicoloured and variegated New Guinea hybrids. All have erect fleshy stems bearing brilliant 3–5cm (1–2in) spurred flowers. Plants may be potted up and overwintered indoors.

Plant type: Tender perennial, normally grown as half-hardy annual.

Flowering time: Early summer to early autumn.

Height: 15–45cm (6–18in)

Spread: 15–30cm (6–12in)

Soil: Moist, well-drained with added humus.

Positioning: Cool shade, 15–23cm (6–9in) apart; ideal for growing under trees if watered in dry weather.

Planting time: After last frosts.

Propagation: Surface-sow at 18–20°C (64–68°F) in early spring and prick out before true leaves develop; take cuttings of side-shoots late spring to late summer.

Care: Plants need regular watering in dry weather and benefit from occasional feeding. In autumn pot up New Guinea hybrids early as they are more sensitive to cool damp weather.

Recommended: Many lovely strains, including (in ascending order of height) Super Elfin, Accent, Tempo, Blitz and Deco.

✹✹ 🏺

Plant type: Hardy/half-hardy annual.

Flowering time: Non-flowering; green foliage in summer, and autumn tints.

Height: 60–90cm (2–3ft)

Spread: 45cm (18in)

Soil: Ordinary, well-drained.

Positioning: Full sun or light shade, 60cm (2ft) apart for single plants, 20cm (8in) for hedges.

Planting time: Late spring.

Propagation: Surface-sow at 20°C (68°F) in soil-based compost in late winter or early spring, and prick out into small pots; sow outdoors in mid-spring.

Care: Regualr watering and feeding will produce larger bushes which may be lightly clipped to shape when grown as a low hedge or screen.

Recommended: K. s. childsii and 'Evergreen' (green all season); K. s. trichophylla, (purple, bronze and red in autumn); 'Acapulco Silver', (silver tipped leaves and purple autumn tints).

KOCHIA SCOPARIA TRICOPHYLLA

An important key ingredient of bedding schemes, with neat uniform foliage bushes for planting as central features or as a summer hedge. Some varieties remain a soft green all season, while others develop brilliant autumn tints. (syn. *Bassia scoparia*.)

Lathyrus odoratus Sweet Pea

LATHYRUS ODORATUS 'JET SET MIXED'

Sweet peas are favourites for cut flowers and temporary screens, with shorter kinds for low hedges, hanging baskets and carpet bedding. For the best flowers choose a fragrant variety, pinch tips of seedlings when 10cm (4in) high, and deadhead regularly.

Plant type: Hardy annual.

Flowering time: Early summer to early autumn.

Height: 15cm–2.4m (6in–8ft)

Spread: 15–30cm (6–12in)

Soil: Rich, well-cultivated and free-draining.

Positioning: Full sun, 15–30cm (6–12in) apart.

Planting time: Mid-spring.

Propagation: Sow in pots (some varieties should be soaked first for 24 hours) under glass, in mid-autumn for over-wintering in a cold frame or in late winter in a cool greenhouse; sow outdoors in mid-spring.

Care: Mulch plants with grass clippings to keep roots cool and moist. Water regularly and feed every two weeks. Train tall varieties on canes or netting.

Recommended: Tall – various Spencer, Galaxy and Royal varieties, 'Old-fashioned Mixture' (fragrant); Dwarf – 'Jet Set', 'Snoopea', 'Bijou', 'Little Sweetheart', 'Cupid'.

Lavatera trimestris Annual Mallow

❄❄❄	🏆

Plant type: Hardy annual.

Flowering time: Early summer to mid-autumn.

Height: 50cm–1.2m (20in–4ft)

Spread: 45–60cm (18–24in)

Soil: Light, rich and well-drained.

Positioning: Full sun or light shade, 45–60cm (18–24in) apart.

Planting time: Late spring.

Propagation: Sow in situ in autumn or spring; also under cool glass in early spring, pricking out into small pots. Plants self-sow freely.

Care: For bushy plants thin outdoor sowings early and plant out pot-grown seedlings as soon as they are large enough – thin or overcrowded plants become very tall and leggy. In exposed positions taller plants may need staking. Gather ripe seeds in autumn and scatter immediately where plants are required next spring, or dry and store for next year.

Recommended: 'Loveliness' (pink), 'Silver Cup', 'Ruby Regis' (rose), 'Mont Blanc' (white).

LAVATERA TRIMESTRIS 'SILVER CUP'

This old cottage garden plant is now a choice and bushy annual with richly coloured flowers up to 10cm (4in) across. Mix with border perennials, mass in bold groups or plant as a hedge at the back of beds. Deadhead regularly for best results.

Limonium sinuatum Statice

LIMONIUM SINUATUM THREE DIFFERENT VARIETIES

This is the most popular 'everlasting' flower, attractive when blooming outdoors but also good for cutting when fully open. Hang in bunches to dry in cool shade for indoor decoration. All varieties tolerate dry soils.

Plant type: Half-hardy annual.

Flowering time: Mid-summer to early autumn.

Height: 30–90cm (1–3ft)

Spread: 30cm (12in)

Soil: Light and well-drained.

Positioning: Full sun, 30cm (12in) apart.

Planting time: Late spring or early summer.

Propagation: Sow at 20°C (68°F) in late winter or early spring, and prick out into trays or small pots.

Care: Little special care needed. For very early flowers, sow seeds in late summer for potting up in early autumn into 12cm (5in) pots. Overwinter in a frost-free greenhouse.

Recommended: Tall – 'Forever', 'Formula', 'Pacific' and 'Sunset' mixtures; single-colour varieties such as 'Blue Peter', 'Forever Gold', 'Sunset' (all illustrated); Dwarf – 'Biedermeier' and 'Petite Bouquet' mixtures.

Plant type: Hardy annual.

Flowering time: Early summer to early autumn.

Height: 30–60cm (12–24in)

Spread: 15cm (6in)

Soil: Most kinds if fertile and well-cultivated.

Positioning: Full sun, 8cm (3in) apart.

Planting time: Sow in situ.

Propagation: Normally sown in situ, in lines 10cm (4in) apart or bold masses, in mid-spring; also in mid-summer for late flowering. For very early flowers, sow seeds in divided trays in group of 4-6 seeds to each cell, in early spring. Harden off and plant out unthinned clusters as soon as large enough. Pot up a few in 12cm (5in) pots or containers for sunny patios.

Care: Plants sown in situ are quite undemanding.

Recommended: *L. g.* var. *album* (white), *L. g.* var. *rubrum* (Scarlet Flax), 'Bright Eyes' (white with red centres).

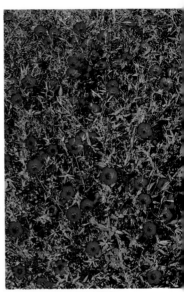

LINUM GRANDIFLORUM VAR. RUBRUM

An easy-going but aristocratic annual to sow lavishly for dramatic impact. Plants bloom continuously over a long season and make excellent cut flowers. Invaluable for filling gaps in borders and for sowing late in pots for autumn displays under glass.

Lobelia erinus Lobelia

LOBELIA ERINUS 'CRYSTAL PALACE'

Once familiar planted with sweet alyssum as formal edging, Lobelia is a brilliant bedding plant in its own right. Trailing kinds may be grown at ground level as well as in containers, and all kinds survive the winter under warm glass to provide cuttings in spring.

Plant type: Tender perennial, grown as half-hardy annual.

Flowering time: Early summer to mid-autumn.

Height: 10–15cm (4–6in)

Spread: 10–30cm (4–12in)

Soil: Moist and fertile best, but tolerates most soils.

Positioning: Full sun or light shade, 15cm (6in) apart.

Planting time: After last frosts.

Propagation: Surface-sow at 18–20°C (64–68°F) in late winter or early spring, and prick out seedlings in small clusters; also take cuttings in spring and plant in heat.

Care: Undemanding.

Recommended: Many kinds including 'Crystal Palace' (dark blue), 'Cambridge Blue' (pale blue), 'Mrs Clibran Improved' (blue with white eye), and red, blue and white mixtures such as 'String of Pearls'; trailing varieties (*L. e.* var. *pendula*) include 'Sapphire' (blue), and 'Cascade' and 'Fountain' blends.

Lobularia maritima Sweet Alyssum, Little Dorrit

Plant type: Hardy annual.

Flowering time: Early summer to mid-autumn.

Height: 8–15cm (3–6in)

Spread: 15–45cm (6–18in)

Soil: Well-drained and not too fertile.

Positioning: Best in full sun but tolerates light shade, 15–20cm (6–8in) apart.

Planting time: Late spring.

Propagation: Sow in a cold frame in late winter and prick out into trays, or sow in situ in mid-spring.

Care: Water regularly in a hot dry season, otherwise plants finish flowering and turn brown. When the main flush of blooms starts to fade, shear them off with scissors and feed to stimulate further growth.

Recommended: White forms include 'Carpet of Snow', 'Snow Crystals', 'Snow Drift'; also 'Rosie O'Day' (pink), 'Oriental Night' (violet-purple) and 'Royal Carpet' (deep purple); 'Pastel Carpet' and 'Wonderland' are fine mixtures.

LOBULARIA MARITIMA 'WONDERLAND'

Little dorrit is just one white variety of sweet alyssum, a favourite annual with honey-scented flowers that self-seeds happily in corners. Pink, red and purple forms are attractive variations on the traditional white ones. (syn. *Alyssum maritimum*.)

MATRICARIA EXIMIA 'GOLDEN BALL'

Confusion reigns over the true botanical name of this popular formal edging plant a cultivated version of feverfew. The foliage is almost unpleasantly pungent, but the pretty white or yellow flowers dry well as everlastings for indoor arrangements. (syn. *Chrysanthemum parthenium*, *Tanacetum parthenium*.)

Plant type: Half-hardy annual.

Flowering time: Mid-summer to mid-autumn.

Height: 15–45cm (6–18in)

Spread: 15–30cm (6–12in)

Soil: Most well-drained soils.

Positioning: Full sun, 15–30cm (6–12in) apart.

Planting time: Late spring or after last frosts.

Propagation: Sow at 20°C (68°F) in late winter or early spring, and prick out into trays.

Care: Occasional watering in dry weather is beneficial and produces larger plants. Most varieties self-seed freely and seedlings can be potted up in autumn, while survivors of winter frosts can be transplanted in spring. Some varieties are tender perennials: pot up in autumn for overwintering in frost-free conditions indoors and divide or take cuttings in spring.

Recommended: 'Butterball', 'Golden Ball', 'Snow Ball'; also *M. grandiflora* 'Gold Pompoms' and 'Pincushion'.

Matthiola incana Stocks

Plant type: Half-hardy annual.
Flowering time: Summer.
Height: 30–60cm (12–24in)
Spread: 23–30cm (9–12in)
Soil: Fertile and well-drained, with a little lime.
Positioning: Full sun or light shade, 23cm (9in) apart.
Planting time: Ten Week Stocks in late spring, East Lothian mid- or late spring.
Propagation: Sow in gentle heat in late winter or early spring, and prick out into pots; sow East Lothian stocks in late summer for over-wintering in a cold frame.
Care: Protect seedlings from slugs. Water plants regularly and feed every two weeks.
Recommended: Ten Week Stocks: various blends including dwarf kinds and earlier flowering 'Trysomic Seven-Week Mixture'; East Lothian: 'Legacy Mixed'; also hardy annual M. bicornis (Night-scented Stock) for sowing broadcast.

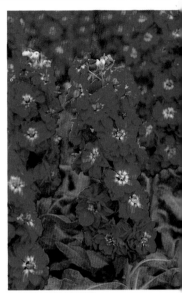

MATTHIOLA INCANA VARIETY

Two main kinds are grown for summer bedding: Ten Week Stocks and East Lothian Stocks (a biennial grown as a half-hardy annual). Mixtures of white, yellow, red and purple usually produce many double flowers; taller kinds are ideal for cutting.

Mimulus × hybridus Monkey Flower

MIMULUA × HYBRIDUS 'MALIBU SERIES'

These bright hybrids are the perfect solution for shade or damp soils, and for filling unexpected gaps – plants flower only 8 weeks after sowing. Deadhead to prolong flowering, and if necessary revive during drought by soaking and lightly trimming plants.

Plant type:	Half-hardy annual.
Flowering time:	Early summer to mid-autumn.
Height:	15–30cm (6–12in)
Spread:	23–30cm (9–12in)
Soil:	Rich soils that do not dry out – moisture is essential.
Positioning:	Full sun or partial shade, 23cm (9in) apart.
Planting time:	After last frosts.
Propagation:	Sow at 21°C (70°F) in mid- to late spring, and barely cover the seeds; prick out into trays or small pots and grow on in cool conditions.
Care:	Regular watering is vital. Plants often tend to sprawl loosely, and benefit from support with twiggy sticks. If flowering ceases halfway through the season, trim plants back to half their height and feed to promote further side-shoots.
Recommended:	Dwarf 'Malibu' and medium height 'Calypso', both mixtures, and tall 'Viva' (yellow with red blotches); single colour selections also available.

Nemesia strumosa Nemesia

Plant type: Half-hardy annual.

Flowering time: Early summer to mid-autumn.

Height: 20–30cm (8–12in)

Spread: 15cm (6in)

Soil: Moist, fairly fertile and lime-free.

Positioning: Full sun (moist soils only) or light shade, 15cm (6in) apart.

Planting time: After last frosts.

Propagation: Sow in frost-free conditions in mid-spring, prick out into trays and grow on fairly cool; in hot dry seasons sow again in mid-summer for continuity.

Care: Little extra care is needed apart from regular watering. If plants finish flowering in a hot season, shear off the top growth to stimulate a second flush of blooms.

Recommended: Mixtures such as 'Carnival', 'Funfair' and 'Tapestry'; single colours 'Fire King' and 'Triumph Red'; bicolors 'KLM' (blue/white) and 'Mello' (red/white); also dwarf *N. nana compacta* 'Orange Prince' and *N. versi-color* 'Blue Gem'.

NEMESIA STRUMOSA 'CARNIVAL MIXED'

The vivid and wildly speckled 2.5cm (1in) blooms guarantee Nemesia's lasting popularity. It is quick to flower, but must be grown in cool conditions at all times, and may need repeat sowing in hot weather.

Nemophila menziesii Baby-Blue-Eyes, Californian Bluebell

Plant type:	Hardy annual.
Flowering time:	Early summer to first frosts.
Height:	10–15cm (4–6in)
Spread:	30cm (12in)
Soil:	Moist and fertile, with plenty of humus.
Positioning:	Full sun or semi-shade, 15cm (6in) apart, as ground cover, as edging and in rock gardens; also suitable for pots and window-boxes
Planting time:	Late spring.
Propagation:	Sow under glass in early spring and prick out into trays, or sow in situ in mid-spring, also in late summer for earlier flowering.
Care:	Prepare soil with leaf mould or garden compost; thin seedlings while small. Water generously when soil is dry for continuous flowers.
Recommended:	Plain species (syn. *N. insignis*); 'Pennie Black' (*N.* var. *discoidalis*), deep blue-purple with white; 'Snowstorm' (*N.* var. *atromaria*), white with black or purple spots; also , *N. maculata* 'Five Spot'.

NEMOPHILIA MENZIESII

A charming and reliable annual that is waiting to be rediscovered – it was once a great favourite for carpet bedding and ground cover under roses. Few plants offer such glorious blue colouring with an indifference to sun or shade.

Nicotiana alata · Tobacco Plant

* ☼

Plant type: Half-hardy annual.

Flowering time: Early summer to mid-autumn.

Height: 25–90cm (10in–3ft)

Spread: 25–45cm (10–18in)

Soil: Any moist but well-drained soil.

Positioning: Full sun or light shade, 25–45cm (10–18in) apart.

Planting time: After last frosts.

Propagation: Surface-sow at 20°C (68°F) in early or mid-spring, prick out while still small and grow on in cool conditions.

Care: Water occasionally in dry weather and stake taller varieties, especially in exposed gardens. Watch out for greenfly and spray if plants are heavily infested. Plants often self-seed, or gather seedpods in early autumn for drying.

Recommended: Various hybrid series such as 'Domino', 'Nikki', 'Roulette', 'Sensation' and 'VIP', as mixtures or single colours; 'Lime Green' (yellowish-green); also N. affinis (syn. N. alata grandiflora), white, very fragrant.

NICOTIANA ALATA 'DOMINO WHITE'

Some of the powerful fragrance has been lost from modern Nicotiana hybrids, but in compensation the blooms often remain open all day and some face upwards, colours are brighter and more weather-resistant, and plants are sturdier and very uniform in height.

Nigella damascena Love-in-a-Mist

NIGELLA DAMASCENA 'MISS JEKYLL'

An old cottage garden annual, with blue, pink or white flowers nestling among finely cut leaves. The display lasts for 6–8 weeks, so deadhead blooms or make a further sowing or two for continuity, especially to fill unexpected gaps in displays.

Plant type: Hardy annual.
Flowering time: Summer and autumn.
Height: 15–75cm (6–30in)
Spread: 15–30cm (6–12in)
Soil: Well-drained with plenty of humus.
Positioning: Full sun or light shade, 20cm (8in) apart.
Planting time: Late spring.
Propagation: Sow in situ in early spring or early autumn, and again in late spring for continuity; sow also in small paper pots (they do not like to be transplanted) in a cold frame in early spring. Gather seedpods as they ripen and scatter seeds wherever more plants are required. A sequence of self-sown plants will gradually establish without the need to sow more.
Care: Undemanding if watered in dry weather and fed occasionally.
Recommended: 'Persian Jewels' is the standard mixture; blue varieties include 'Dwarf Moody Blue', 'Miss Jekyll', 'Oxford Blue' and 'Shorty Blue'; also 'Miss Jekyll Alba' (white) and 'Mulberry Rose' (deep pink).

Papaver rhoeas Annual Poppy, Corn Poppy

Plant type: Hardy annual or biennial.

Flowering time: Early summer to early autumn.

Height: 30–90cm (1–3ft)

Spread: 23–30cm (9–12in)

Soil: Fairly fertile and well-cultivated.

Positioning: Full sun or light shade, 20–30cm (8–12in) apart.

Planting time: Mid- to late spring, summer-sown plants in autumn.

Propagation: Best sown in situ, in mid-spring or early autumn. Also sow under cool glass: annuals in early spring and biennials in mid-summer or mid-winter to flower same year; prick out into small pots.

Care: These plants are very undemanding.

Recommended: Champagne Bubbles', 'Wonderland', 'San Remo' and 'Garden Gnome', mixtures, and 'Matador' (scarlet); and 'Mother of Pearl', 'Shirley Double'; 'Paeony-flowered Mixture', 'Pink Chiffon', also *Papaver nudicaule* (Iceland Poppy).

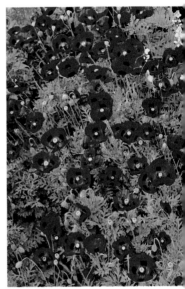

PAPAVER RHOEAS 'LADYBIRD'

Dainty and graceful though they look fluttering in the summer breeze, poppies are tough and reliable plants with large single or double flowers, in vivid or subtle pastel colours according to variety. Many are also excellent as cut flowers.

PELARGONIUM HORTORUM 'DECORA LILAS'

The classic bedding plant, now available in many colours and forms – sturdy and large-flowered zonal geraniums; prolific or small-flowered floribundas; and trailing ivy-leaved varieties such as 'Maverick Scarlet' and 'Decora Lilas' (above) for baskets and ground cover.

Plant type: Tender perennial.

Flowering time: Early summer to mid-autumn, later under glass.

Height: 23–45cm (9–18in)

Spread: 23–45cm (9–18in)

Soil: Rich and well-drained.

Positioning: Full sun or very light shade, 23–30cm (9–12in) apart.

Planting time: After last frosts.

Propagation: Sow at 24°C (75°F) under glass in mid- to late winter, prick out into small pots and grow on in cool conditions, potting on as plants develop; also take cuttings in mid- to late summer.

Care: These plants are very undemanding.

Recommended: Hundreds of good named varieties; also 'Breakaway', 'Carioca', 'Gala', 'Multibloom', 'Pulsar', 'Sprinter', and 'Startel' zonal mixtures; Trailing *P. peltatum*, with numerous named kinds including 'Cascade' and 'Harlequin' series, plus 'Summer Showers' and 'Tornado' seed mixtures.

Plant type:	Tender perennial, grown as half-hardy annual.
Flowering time:	Early summer to early autumn.
Height:	15–45cm (6–18in)
Spread:	20–30cm (8–12in)
Soil:	Light, rich and well-drained.
Positioning:	Full sun, 23–30cm (9–12in) apart.
Planting time:	After last frosts.
Propagation:	Surface-sow at 24°C (75°F) under glass mid-winter to early spring, prick out into trays and then pot up individually; also cuttings in spring from overwintered plants.
Care:	These plants are very undemanding.
Recommended:	Multiflora series include 'Celebrity', 'Plum Pudding' and 'Resisto'; Grandifloras 'Colour Parade', 'Daddy', 'Merlin' and 'Picotee'; Miniature 'Fantasy Junior'; Trailing (P. pendula) – 'Cascade', 'Super-cascade', 'Purple Wave' and also 'Million Bells' and 'Surfinia' series (both plants only).

PETUNIA HYBRIDA 'PURPLE WAVE'

A wide range of colours, markings and forms (single, double and ruffled) has made petunias a favourite for bedding and container culture. Plants prefer hot dry weather and may disappoint in a wet season, although some kinds are more weather-resistant.

Phacelia campanularia Phacelia

PHACELIA CAMPANULARIA 'BLUE BONNET'

Good blue bedding plants are rare, and Phacelia is worth growing just for its intense gentian-blue flowers. It is very easily raised, flowering in just 8 weeks over a long period, and thrives on the poorest soils, while also making a spectacular pot plant.

Plant type:	Hardy annual.
Flowering time:	Mid-summer to early autumn.
Height:	23–30cm (9–12in)
Spread:	15cm (6in)
Soil:	Light, poor and well-drained.
Positioning:	Full sun or light shade, 15cm (6in) apart.
Planting time:	Late spring.
Propagation:	Sow in situ in autumn or early spring; also in small pots in a cold frame in early spring.
Care:	The young seedlings are very vulnerable, and need protection against cats and birds, and later against slugs. A hot summer may curtail flowering; water thoroughly whenever dry as an insurance, and in early summer start a further batch in cell trays for planting out without root disturbance.
Recommended:	Normal species; also larger flowered 'Tropical Surf' and taller 'Blue Bonnet'; *P. dubia* 'Lavender Lass' is similar, ideal for heavy soils; also *P. parryi* and its selection 'Royal Admiral'.

Phlox drummondii Annual Phlox

Plant type: Hardy or half-hardy annual.

Flowering time: Early summer to early autumn.

Height: 10–45cm (4–18in)

Spread: 10–20cm (4–8in)

Soil: Fertile and moisture-retentive but well-drained.

Positioning: Full sun, 15–20cm (6–8in) apart.

Planting time: Late spring.

Propagation: Sow at 13°C (55°F) in early spring in soil-based compost and prick out into trays, or sow in situ mid- to late spring.

Care: Protect the young plants against slugs (wild rabbits are also very fond of phlox blooms). If flowering stops in a hot season, shear off the faded blooms to promote side-shoots.

Recommended: Tall – 'Brilliant' (rose with white eye), 'Phlox of Sheep' and various 'Large-flowered' or 'Choice' mixtures. Dwarf – 'Beauty', 'Chanal', 'Ethnie Pastel Shades', 'Promise Peach' and 'Twinkles'.

PHLOX DRUMMONDII 'TWINKLE STAR DWARF MIXED'

Modern selections and hybrids have transformed the old untidy annual into a wonderful range of neat and brilliant bedding plants, the taller varieties equally good for cutting. Easy to grow if you avoid slugs and over-watering.

Portulaca grandiflora Sun Plant

PORTULACA GRANDIFLORA 'CALYPSO MIXED'

Mats of spreading succulent foliage, with brilliant displays of colour all summer in dry sunny positions. Older forms close their blooms in dull or wet weather, but new kinds are an improvement. Pot up a few plants for a sunny window-sill.

Plant type: Half-hardy annual.

Flowering time: Early summer to early autumn.

Height: 10–20cm (4–8in)

Spread: 30cm (12in)

Soil: Light, dry and well-drained.

Positioning: Full sun, 15–30cm (6–12in) apart.

Planting time: After last frosts.

Propagation: Sow at 13°C (55°F) in late winter and early spring, and barely cover seeds; prick out into small pots at three-leaf stage.

Care: Plants are quite fussy about growing conditions, and dislike heavy soils and wet positions. Do not over-water seedlings as they are susceptible to damping-off disease, and the same applies to established plants, which should only be watered if they look distressed.

Recommended: 'Cloudbeater Mixed' (flowers remain open in dull weather), 'Kariba Mixed', 'Sundance', 'Sundial', 'Swanlake' (double white).

Ricinus communis Castor Oil Plant

*

Plant type: Tender perennial, often grown as half-hardy annual.

Flowering time: Mid-summer.

Height: 90cm–1.8m (3–6ft), more in warm climates.

Spread: 60cm (2ft)

Soil: Any garden soil.

Positioning: Full sun, as a 'dot' or foliage plant; not for cold or exposed gardens.

Planting time: Late spring or early summer.

Propagation: Sow single seeds in small pots in early spring, under glass at 21°C (70°F).

Care: Keep seedlings warm and move into larger pots as necessary, supporting taller plants with canes. Harden off fully before planting out. Stake tall varieties securely, water in dry weather and feed every 2–3 weeks with a general fertilizer.

Recommended: 'Carmencita' (deep brown leaves, red flowers); 'Impala' (maroon leaves, sulphur yellow flowers); 'Zanzibarensis' (bronze, green and purple leaves, white veins, tall).

RICINUS COMMUNIS 'IMPALA'

A popular and imposing foliage plant with glistening coloured leaves up to 50cm (20in) in length. In a warm conservatory it will grow into a shrub or small tree, but it is usually raised annually from seed for use as a 'dot' or container plant. Note: the seed coats are very poisonous.

Rudbeckia hirta Cone Flower

RUDBECKIA HIRTA 'RUSTIC DWARFS'

Late-flowering and prolific, these bold daisies glow with dramatic autumn shades of gold, cinnamon, mahogany and nutmeg, each bloom with a prominent central cone. In mild gardens plants may survive as short-lived perennials.

Plant type: Hardy or half-hardy annual.

Flowering time: Late summer to mid-autumn.

Height: 30–90cm (1–3ft)

Spread: 30cm (12in)

Soil: Fertile and well-drained.

Positioning: Full sun or light shade, 30cm (12in) apart.

Planting time: Late spring.

Propagation: Sow in gentle heat or a cold frame in early spring, and prick out into trays or small pots.

Care: Protect young plants against slugs. Water and feed regularly during the growing period from planting out until flowering begins in late summer: strong well-branched bushes give the best displays. Stake taller varieties.

Recommended: 'Giant Tetraploid Mixed', 'Gloriosa Daisies', 'Goldilocks', 'Irish Eyes' (yellow with green centres), 'Kelvedon Star', 'Marmalade', 'Nutmeg', 'Rustic Dwarf Mixed'.

Salpiglossis sinuata Painted Tongue, Trumpet Flower

❋ ▽

Plant type: Half-hardy annual.
Flowering time: Mid-summer to early autumn.
Height: 45–90cm (18in–3ft)
Spread: 45cm (18in)
Soil: Rich and well-drained; avoid dry or waterlogged soils.
Positioning: Sunny sheltered positions, 23cm (9in) apart.
Planting time: Early summer.
Propagation: Sow at 15°C (60°F) in mid-spring and barely cover seeds; prick out at three-leaf stage into small pots. Save some seeds for sowing under glass in early autumn for winter flowering.
Care: Water seedlings carefully as they are prone to damping-off disease, and harden off thoroughly before planting out. All but the shortest varieties benefit from some kind of support, and you should also check plants regularly for aphids.
Recommended: 'Bolero Mixed', 'Casino Mixed', 'Festival', 'Flamenco', 'Gloomy Rival' (unusual grey and chocolate combination).

SALPIGLOSSIS SINUATA VARIETY

Exotic and eye-catching trumpet flowers in bright colours with intricate contrasting veins, rather like extravagant Alstroemerias. Try them as cut flowers and pot plants in a cool conservatory, supporting the slender flower stems with twiggy sticks.

Salvia splendens Salvia, Scarlet Sage

SALVIA SPLENDENS 'SALSA SCARLET'

A constant favourite, salvias were once only fiery red but new strains include lovely shades of white, pink, apricot and purple. Other Salvias grown for bedding include blue forms and the drought-tolerant clary with its showy red, blue and white bracts.

Plant type: Tender perennial, grown as half-hardy annual.

Flowering time: Early summer to mid-autumn.

Height: 20–60cm (8–24in)

Spread: 20–30cm (8–12in)

Soil: Most kinds if fertile and well-drained.

Positioning: Full sun, 23cm (9in) apart.

Planting time: After last frosts.

Propagation: Sow at 21°C (70°F) in late winter and early spring, and prick out into small pots; for bushy plants pinch out tips of seedlings.

Care: Undemanding. Dead-head occasionally to stimulate side-shoots.

Recommended: Many kinds, including 'Blaze of Fire', 'Dress Parade', 'Firecracker', 'Laser Purple', 'Phoenix Mixed', 'Red Arrow', 'Salsa Scarlet', 'Splendissima' and 'Vanguard'; also *S. coccinea* 'Cherry Blossom' and 'Lady in Red'; *S. horminum* (Clary) 'Claryssa'; *S. farinacea* 'Silver' and 'Victoria' (violet); *S. patens* (blue).

✳✳

Plant type:	Hardy or half-hardy annual.
Flowering time:	Mid-summer to early autumn.
Height:	45–90cm (18–36in)
Spread:	30cm (12in)
Soil:	Rich and well-drained, with a little lime.
Positioning:	Full sun, 23–30cm (9–12in) apart.
Planting time:	Late spring; early spring for overwintered plants.
Propagation:	Sow at 21°C (70°F) in early spring and prick out into small pots, or sow in a cold frame in mid-summer and overwinter for earlier flowers.
Care:	Little special care needed. Do not over-water, but feed plants occasionally and support taller varieties in exposed gardens or in a prolonged wet season.
Recommended:	'Double Mixed', 'Dwarf Double Mixed', 'Giant Hybrids Mixed', 'Butterfly'; also *S. stellata* 'Drumstick', 'Paper Moon' or 'Sternkugel' (blue flowers with bronze spherical seedheads for drying).

SCABIOSA ATROPURPUREA 'BUTTERFLY BLUE'

An easy and colourful annual for filling summer gaps in beds and borders, and also sown in rows for cutting. Plants need a long growing season, and are best sown early the same year or overwintered from a late sowing. Some varieties are very fragrant.

SCHIZANTHUS PINNATUS

With shelter and good drainage this lives up to its common name, the striking flowers in many colours resembling small orchids. For outdoor use choose compact varieties, reserving the tall kinds as exciting pot plants for the conservatory.

Plant type:	Half-hardy annual.
Flowering time:	Mid- and late summer.
Height:	15–45cm (6–18in)
Spread:	15–30cm (6–12in)
Soil:	Light, fertile and very well-drained.
Positioning:	Full sun with shelter from winds, 23cm (9in) apart.
Planting time:	After last frosts.
Propagation:	Sow at 21°C (70°F) in early spring and barely cover seeds; prick out into small pots (2–3 seedlings in each) and grow on in cool conditions. May also be sown under glass in late summer to flower in pots early the following spring.
Care:	For the best-shaped plants, pinch out the growing tip when the stem is about 7cm (3in) high and repeat occasionally with the side-shoots. Water and feed regularly as growth develops, but guard against over-watering because plants seldom recovers.
Recommended:	'Angel Wings', 'Disco', 'Dwarf Bouquet', 'Hit Parade', 'Magnum Hybrids' (tall), 'Star Parade'.

Senecio cineraria Dusty Miller

Plant type:	Tender perennial, grown as half-hardy annual.
Flowering time:	Foliage plant, used from late spring to mid-autumn.
Height:	20–45cm (8–18in)
Spread:	15–30cm (6–12in)
Soil:	Any ordinary well-drained soil.
Positioning:	Full sun, 15–25cm (6–10in) apart.
Planting time:	Late spring.
Propagation:	Sow in gentle heat in early spring and prick out into trays, or in situ in late spring; take cuttings in spring or autumn.
Care:	Undemanding once established. Water young plants regularly and guard against slugs. In mild conditions plants may survive the winter as perennials, especially if protected with cloches against excessive dampness. Alternatively, pot up and keep on the dry side in a frost-free greenhouse for cuttings in spring.
Recommended:	'Cirrus', 'Silver Dust' (dwarf, finely cut leaves).

SENECIO CINERARIA 'CIRRUS'

The perfect contrast and foil for bright bedding plants, dusty miller has two forms, both with silvery-white foliage, and small yellow flowers that should be removed. The compact 'Silver Dust' is the one usually grown for intricate bedding schemes or edging. (syn. *S. bicolor, S. maritima, Cineraria maritima*.)

TAGETES PATULA 'ALAMO GOLD FLAME'

The *Tagetes* family is indispensable, including both French and African marigolds and pretty small-flowered *Tagetes* varieties. They are the main source of yellow and gold in bedding schemes, but fine reds and autumn colours are also available in modern varieties.

Plant type: Half-hardy annual.

Flowering time: Early summer to mid-autumn.

Height: 15–60cm (6–24in)

Spread: 15–30cm (6–12in)

Soil: Any fertile, well-drained soil.

Positioning: Full sun, 10–20cm (4–8in) apart.

Planting time: After last frosts.

Propagation: Sow at 13°C (55°F) in early spring and prick out into trays.

Care: Very easily grown if watered in dry weather, especially in first half of summer. Some varieties may need deadheading.

Recommended: Many kinds including 'Bonita Mixed', 'Alamo', 'Favourite Mixed', 'Golden Gate', 'Honeycomb', 'Naughty Marietta', 'Queen Series', 'Spanish Brocade' and 'Susie Wong'; also *T. erecta* (African Marigold) 'Crackerjack', 'Galore Hybrids', 'Inca', 'Sunset Giants', 'Toreador Hybrids'; *T. signata pumila* (Tagetes) 'Gem Series', 'Paprika', 'Starfire'.

Thunbergia alata Black-eyed Susan

Plant type: Half-hardy annual climber.

Flowering time: Mid-summer to early autumn.

Height: 1.2–3m (4–10ft)

Spread: 45–60cm (18–24in)

Soil: Ordinary, well-drained.

Positioning: Full sun, 45cm (18in) apart, to climb up posts and trellis, or trail from hanging baskets.

Planting time: After last frosts.

Propagation: Sow at 21°C (70°F) in early spring, transplant seedlings to small pots and pot on later.

Care: Very easy to grow. Harden off thoroughly before planting out, water regularly and feed every fortnight for the best displays. The vigorous species will need strong support on trellis or wires, while more restrained varieties can be left to twine into adjacent plants or trail on the ground.

Recommended: Basic species or more restrained 'Susie Mixed'; also *T. fragrans* 'Angel Wings' (white flowers with yellow eyes).

THUNBERGIA ALATA 'SUSIE'

A vigorous climber or trailing plant with lush attractive foliage and conspicuous flowers that are white, yellow or orange, all with a clear deep purple throat. Exotic in appearance, it needs shelter outdoors and makes an excellent plant for the conservatory.

Tropaeolum majus Nasturtium

TROPAEOLUM MAJUS 'ALASKA MIXED'

A blaze of rich colour is guaranteed from these sun-loving annuals with edible leaves, flowers and seeds (pickled as capers). Compact forms are ideal for carpet bedding, taller kinds for summer screens or as wide-spreading imaginative ground cover.

Plant type: Hardy annual.

Flowering time: Early summer to early autumn.

Height: 15cm–2.4m (6in–8ft)

Spread: 20–60cm (8–24in)

Soil: Light and well-drained, with low fertility.

Positioning: Full sun or partial shade, 20cm (8in) apart.

Planting time: Late spring.

Propagation: Sow under cool glass in late winter, 2–3 seeds to each small pot, or sow outdoors in mid-spring where plants are to grow.

Care: Undemanding. Water in very dry seasons.

Recommended: Tall – 'Climbing Jewel of Africa' (variegated), 'Tall Mixed Hybrids'; Dwarf – 'Alaska Mixed' (variegated), '(Double) Gleam Hybrids', 'Empress of India' (crimson), 'Peach Melba' (red/yellow), 'Tom Thumb Mixed', 'Vesuvius' (dark leaves), 'Whirlbird' (upward-facing and spurless); also *T. peregrinum* (Canary Creeper), yellow annual climber.

Venidium fastuosum
Monarch of the Veldt, Cape Daisy

Plant type:	Half-hardy annual.
Flowering time:	Mid-summer to mid-autumn.
Height:	45–60cm (18–24in)
Spread:	45cm (18in)
Soil:	Light and well-drained.
Positioning:	Full sun, 30cm (12in) apart.
Planting time:	After last frosts.
Propagation:	Sow at 10°C (50°F) in early or mid-spring in well-drained soil-based compost, barely covering the seeds. Prick out into small pots.
Care:	Do not over-water the seedlings as they rot easily. Keep cool and well-lit as they develop, but shield them from hot sun until growing strongly. Flowering plants need little care, apart from occasional watering in very dry seasons. Avoid over-watering.
Recommended:	Basic species, and 'Zulu Prince' (contrasting silvery foliage).

VENIDIUM FASTUOSUM

Sometimes included in *Arctotis*, this is a proud and glorious 'daisy', easily grown and ideal for hot dry beds. The striking 10cm (4in) flowers tend to close in dull weather, but are a vivid sight in full sun and also good for cutting.

Verbena hybrida Verbena

VERBENA HYBRIDA 'QUARTZ MIXED'

The low spreading habit of most Verbenas suits them to hanging baskets, window-boxes and other containers, which benefit from their non-stop flowering. Just pinch the tips of young plants for bushy growth, deadhead now and then, and water regularly.

Plant type:	Tender perennial, grown as half-hardy annual.
Flowering time:	Early summer to mid-autumn.
Height:	15–45cm (6–18in)
Spread:	15–45cm (6–18in)
Soil:	Fertile and well-drained.
Positioning:	Full sun, 30cm (12in) apart.
Planting time:	After last frosts.
Propagation:	Sow at 21°C (70°F) in early spring, and transplant to small pots; take cuttings from mature plants in early autumn. Plants may be potted up in autumn for overwintering in a warm dry place to provide cuttings the following spring.
Care:	This plant is very undemanding.
Recommended:	'Dwarf Jewels', 'Mamuth Formula', 'Olympia', 'Quartz', 'Peaches & Cream', 'Showtime', 'Springtime' (all mixtures), and single colours such as 'Amethyst', 'Blaze' (scarlet), 'Blue Lagoon', 'Romance Lavender'; also *V. venosa* (syn. *V. rigida*), violet-purple.

Viola × wittrockiana Pansy

Plant type: Hardy perennial, grown as half-hardy annual.

Flowering time: Late spring to mid-autumn.

Height: 15–25cm (6–10in)

Spread: Up to 30cm (12in)

Soil: Deep, rich and moist.

Positioning: Full sun or light shade, 20cm (8in) apart.

Planting time: Late spring.

Propagation: Sow at 21°C (70°F) from late winter to mid-spring, prick out into small pots and grow on in very cool conditions; take cuttings in late summer and plant in a cold frame.

Care: Little care needed.

Recommended: Many summer varieties, including 'Clear Crystals', 'Swiss Giants', 'Water Colours' (all mixtures), and separates 'Jolly Joker' (blue/orange), 'Padparadja' (orange), 'Rippling Waters' (purple/white), 'Ullswater Blue'; also small-flowered violas V. cornuta (syn. V. hybrida) such as 'Arkwright Ruby', 'Baby Lucia' and 'Chantreyland'.

VIOLA × WITTROCKIANA 'JOKER LIGHT BLUE'

Winter pansies have stolen the limelight from their summer cousins, which boast the longest flowering season of all bedding plants. The range is enormous, and as they are perennials they may be perpetuated from cuttings.

Zinnia hybrida Zinnia

ZINNIA HYBRIDA

Unfairly branded as temperamental, zinnias are easy to grow if given warm soils and sunshine. There are many kinds, from open daisies like single chrysanthemums to fat pompons, ranging in height between tall cutting varieties and compact dwarfs.

Plant type: Half-hardy annual.
Flowering time: Mid-summer to mid-autumn.
Height: 15–90cm (6in–3ft)
Spread: 15–30cm (6–12in)
Soil: Deep, rich and moisture-retentive.
Positioning: Full sun with shelter from wind, 15–30cm (6–12in) apart.
Planting time: Early summer.
Propagation: Sow at 13°C (55°F) in early spring to give plants a long growing season. Avoid over-watering, and always prick out into small pots as plants dislike disturbance. Sow in situ in late spring.
Care: Pinch out growing tips to induce bushy growth.
Recommended: Tall – 'Chippendale' (yellow-edged) 'Giant Cactus-flowered Mixed', 'Scabious-flowered Mixed', 'State Fair Mixed'; Short – 'Early Wonder Mixed', 'Envy' (green), 'Hobgoblin', 'Persian Carpet', 'Peter Pan', 'Thumbelina Mixed'.